MW00892420

First published by Pen & Possum Productions, LLC
Hinton, WV

Pen & Possum
Productions

ISBN: 9798334244993

Call of the Whip-poor-will

Poems, Songs, and a Small History

by Christine Lowry

About the Author

Mary Christine Lowry was born in 1920 and lived her entire life in the mountains of WV. She was one of 15 children, had four children of her own with her husband, Thomas, and had a lasting impact on everyone who knew and loved her. Like many of the women of her generation, she did a little bit of everything – cooking, baking, farming, gardening, quilting, teaching, and caring for anyone within reach. This book is an attempt to put as many of her poems, stories, drawings, and little bits of her, together to share with family, friends, and the world. Christine died on January 27, 2021 at the age of 100.

Note from the Editor

Christine Lowry wrote everything in beautiful cursive handwriting. Sometimes, she would revise pieces, particularly pieces that celebrated holidays or special events. I have tried to select the most recent version of pieces to include in this compilation. I have also tried to faithfully follow her punctuation in poetry. Some of her papers would include doodles as she planned quilts based on her drawings and some of those have been included as pictures.

Cover Art

A Family History
The Sawmill Camp

I'm positively certain that the first remembrance I have of my childhood was in a sawmill camp in Mercer County near Flat Top. The camp was known simply as Toad Level and where the name originated, I never knew. There were several shanties all alike side by side in a row facing the sawmill. At the head of the row and the largest one was the boarding house where an assortment of men of all ages stayed, worked on the mill and ate their dinner at a long table in the Big Kitchen. On the upper side of the kitchen were the living quarters of old Mrs. Gresham who kept the boarding house. Even my earliest memory of her, she seemed old with her long dresses and early American sun bonnet. She was very prim and proper and very religious and we kids were very much in awe of her, even though she made the best thick sweet cakes ever. She cooked, cleaned, and talked to herself. She couldn't read cursive but could read print. She was seldom without her Bible in leisure hours.

At the bottom of the row of shanties was the commissary or camp store. It smelled very much of cigar smoke and tobacco. But the shelves were full of good things and we kids liked to be able to go at nighttime for some errand, where all gathered after work to talk shop. There, Billy Burks, owner of the mill, kept the ledger where all the work hours were kept and the groceries were charged against the paycheck. He went to Flat Top two or three times a week and brought the mail for everyone and put it in a wooden box nailed to the wall. He owned the mill and all the camp shanties, boarding houses, and stores. But my Dad [*Minor Hodge*] was the sawyer at the mill and straw boss and we thought he was very important. We owned two acres of ground and a five-room house so that made us a little better than the general row of kids that moved in and out of the shanties (or so we thought).

Our house was out of sight of the mill, but not too far but what we heard was the chug, chug of the mill and could see the smoke boil out of the stack, and I'm sure the greatest thrill of my young life was the whistle on the steam boiler that blew at 7 in the morning, at exactly 12 noon not five minutes early or late, but precisely on the dot, and again at six, winter and summer. During the summer, my brother and I always lit out running at the noon whistle, to meet my Dad to walk him home to lunch.

He'd never take us by the hand but hold down a big finger for us to grasp. He was a big man, kind and gentle, but made of steel when necessary and also had a violent temper when provoked. He resembled strength and security to us then and we were as proud to walk him home as if he'd been president. As far back as I can remember, he had half a nail on the third finger of his left hand where he'd mashed it with a log years before and when he went to his grave in 1960, it was still the same. He was sawmill man first, last, and always and could tell from the whine of the saw even as a violinist listens to the strings if all was well and it had to be perfect for him.

Sawmill ca1911. Minor located far right.

My Sawmill Shack in WV (unfinished)
Written for Nelson Lowry

Oh, I want to go back to my sawmill shack
In the hills of WV
To the little old sawmill shack
Where I was born.
It was early in the morn, the
Day that I was born
In the hills of WV, far away.

The snow was on the ground
But the moon shone big
On the morn that I was born in WV.

I remember yet the day tho
The years have rolled away
Since the morn that
I was born in WV.

Minor Crayton Hodge Meets Cora Pitzer

He [*Minor Hodge*] told us tales of his childhood. He was born in Ohio. He had an assortment of stepmothers as his real mother died when he was very small. He said once when he was about 8 or 10, his puppy ran away and someone told him if he'd grease its feet with lard, it would stay home. It was Sunday and his stepmother had a white counterpane on her spare bed, but that was where he set the dog to grease his feet, and I think, he and doggie both almost had to leave home.

His first sawmill, he built himself with his brothers' help. They used an 8-gallon lard can for a steam boiler, built the engine of odds and ends, and used his suspenders for a belt to turn the wheels. Needless to say, that

Minor Crayton Hodge,
Age Unknown

one ended in disaster. He bought his first real one at the age of 16 and was in the business until about 2 years before he died. He came to WVa from Ohio on the last day of December 1906. It was midnight when his train stopped at Hinton, and it was raining bullfrogs. He spent the night at the YMCA. He had a cousin named Johnny Boland, who had a sawmill operation in Summers County, so that's where he headed.

And it wasn't very long till "The Sawmill Boys" as they were known began to attend dances in the parlors of the folks around the countryside and there my dad met the

11

black-haired, black-eyed maiden who fate had chosen to be his wife and my mother. When she first saw him in the crowd, she asked her dancing partner who the new fellow was. He answered Minor Hodge. Her first remark was, "What a funny name, and, gee, ain't he ugly?"

She was 16 and the belle of every ball and had beaus by the dozen, but either my dad was impressed by her indifference, or she wanted to find out what made him tick. That night marked the beginning of a stormy courtship, and they were married in a year or so on July 1, 1908, just before her eighteenth birthday.

Cora Belle Pitzer, Age unknown

She was the baby of the family and maybe spoiled and my dad was still young and wild and didn't settle down right away. He'd forget and get drunk on payday and she'd cry and go home to Grandma. When he sobered up, he'd swear on the Bible never to get drunk again and so went the first few years.

Cora and Minor

Mommy's Light
1942

When day is done, with its toil and cares,
And the sun has sunk from sight,
Far out, like a beacon in the dark,
Shines the rays of Mommy's light.

Like a lighthouse built upon the sand,
Shining far out, on the ocean's foam,
So, Mommy's lamp lights up the path,
That leads the way back home.

Sometimes the fog is thick and dark,
The world is cold and damp,
But I know behind the mist and form,
Still glistens Mommy's lamp.

When Mommy's lamp, down here on earth,
Shall shine no more at night,
I know from her window in Heaven,
Will still glisten, Mommy's lamp.

The Children Start Coming

In four years of marriage, they borned and buried three tiny premature sons. Three doctors on their lack of medical knowledge told them they'd never have a child to live. They were unhappy and almost came to parting of the ways. But in August 1912, they had a little girl (Bernice) and their luck changed for fast. After her came another son (Ted, 1914) and daughter (Irene 1915) and still another stillborn son to make the little graves on the hillside number four and read, Tommy Thompson Hodge, John Hodge, Joe Hodge, and last George Milton Hodge.

In another year, another son (Billie, September 25, 1918) and in a couple of years, I was born (November 19, 1920)! The ninth child in their 12 years of marriage, I was scrawny and blue and stubborn and tried not to live, but at six months, I took whooping cough, which wore down whatever resentment I

Cora holding Christine, ca1921

had at life, and I gave up fighting and decided to stay around and see what was going on.

I was followed by two more brothers (Alvie 1922 and Paul 1926) and four sisters (Betty 1924, Bonnie 1929, Melva 1931, and Leola 1933). Thirteen more years, which ended my mom's years of fruitfulness as far as childbearing was concerned and if some of the older ones hadn't left to start homes and families of their own, we'd sure would've had to build a bigger table. For in all the places we lived through, which numbered at least 25, I think we moved the same table and long bench that went with it where all the younger ones lined up to eat, for that bench held 4, 5, 6 people depending on their size and ability to share. After the last one left home, Dad cut it down to two feet to make Mom a flower bench. I still have it though, and am glad it can't talk for it could tell even more tales on that family that I could or would dare to.

We owned, beside the house, barn, garden, and cow pasture at Flat Top in Mercer County, a two-acre farm with the same amount of outbuildings on top of outbuildings on top of Elk Knob Mountain in Summers County. There, my maternal grandparents lived in an old log house with a huge fireplace and a small lean-to kitchen, and a stairway going

16

up on the outside. Granny Pitzer was tall as nearly any man I knew, six feet to be exact, and Grandad was 5 ½ feet, a dapper little dandy with silver hair and a mustache to match. He always rode horseback and wore leather leggings, which gave him a bow-legged look (or he probably was). He wore spurs too that jingled when he walked. He was full of mischief and always played jokes on everyone. They were kind and good to everyone and were affectionately known as Uncle Tom and Aunt Betty to all the neighbors. Grandad died of dropsy when I was eight; he was 75 and had been an invalid for a year. I remember the night he lay a corpse. The neighbors sat and sang hymns for hours and the older gentlemen asked for salt to lick. My older brother was 16 and thought he was man of the world. He and a meaner cousin of 25 or more sat in the kitchen and made fun of the singers. After his death, Granny broke up housekeeping and the big old clock that had set on the mantel over the fireplace swinging its pendulum to and fro, so many years went with her. She came to us from time to time but because we were so many and we were always more on the way, and we moved so much to follow the timber trail that she didn't visit us too often.

Amazing Grace
1972

"Amazing Grace, how sweet the sound,
That saved a wretch like me.
I once was lost but now I'm found,
Was blind but now I see."

When I was a little child, I knelt at Mother's knee.
She told me how Christ was once a little child like me.
She told me many stories, that I'd love to hear again,
Then Mama shouted, sister prayed, and Daddy said Amen.

Then Dad would take the Bible down and read it just for me.
He read about how Moses walked across the great Red Sea.
He read about how Daniel prayed while in the lion's den,
Then Mama shouted, sister prayed, and Daddy said Amen.

Then Mama would sing a song for me that told of God's great
plan,
And how he sent his only son to rescue fallen man.
She told how Jesus died to save my soul from sin,
Then Mama shouted, sister prayed, and Daddy said Amen.

I wish that I could go again, back to the old home place,
To hear again my Daddy's voice and see my Mama's face.
But I believe that I shall see my loved ones once again,
Hear Mama shout, and sister pray, and Daddy say Amen.

"In the sweet by and by,
We shall meet on that beautiful shore,
In the sweet by and by,
We shall meet on that beautiful shore."

Bernice and Irene

There were seven of us girls and all are living except the youngest who died in 1936. (*Editor's Note – Christine wrote this family history in the 1980s. All of the siblings are now deceased.*)

Bernice was the oldest of the seven, and the rest of us sort of looked up to her. She was our substitute mother when Mom wasn't around, and she did lots of nice things for all of us. She was a shy and nervous type, and I can remember her crying so many times when I wasn't old enough to know what there was to cry about. But she was tender-hearted and very sensitive and life wasn't very kind to poor people those days. She was married at a very early age to Ray Hodge, a third cousin. They bore and raised twelve children. All but one graduated from high school and every son of them joined the army (8 boys to be exact). Several of them were paratroopers; some of them made Army a career. Only one was unable to be a solder. Ray died of cancer and Bernice lives in NC near the army base where some of her sons live. (*Editor's note: Bernice died in 1988.*)

Irene came next. She was born in 1915. She was the quiet turned one, and wasn't a tom-boy like me. She was a house person, first, last, and always. She kept the house straight and everything folded and in its proper place. She sewed and embroidered and did the ironing. She loved to sleep better than anyone, and when the weather was cold, she'd go to bed in a coat, socks, and toboggan if Mom didn't catch her. She stayed with elderly people to help out while still very young. She would always buy all of us something when she came home. She had long hair all her life and at home, she wore a dust cap. There were pretty little caps with ruffles and Mom made them in pretty colors for herself, Bernice, and Irene. Once Irene and I took a walk and found the nicest patch of raspberries. Having no containers, Irene took off her pretty, light blue dust-cap and we picked it full. Oh, what a disaster! Of course, the cap was ruined, but the pie sure was good.

Irene met Kenton Hartwell and married him in 1932. She was only sixteen and of course, they eloped. They had fifteen children. One died a few after birth (1945), and one son was killed in 1975 in a car accident. Their oldest son died in 1984 of cancer. Kent had a stroke in 1960 and has been semi-invalid. They had their 50th anniversary in 1982 and this year will be their 54th anniversary. They live in the old home place on Zion Mountain. (*Editor's note: Irene died in*

20

2004. Both Kenton and Irene are buried at the cemetery at the end of Hartwell Road near where they lived.)

Christine's Arrival

Next came me in the line of girls. I was born at Flat Top in Mercer County in 1920 – the year Harding was elected president. My parents were died-in-the-wool Republicans and if I'd been a boy, my name was to have been Warren Harding Hodge. I'm sure glad I was a girl. Mary Christine is so much prettier a name. I was named for my mom's older sister, Mary, and for my paternal grandmother, Christina.

Times were hard in our growing years, but we as kids didn't know it. We always had plenty to eat, and enough to wear, trees to climb, wigwams to build, friends in plenty, and each other and life was very good.

The Christmases of our youth were so special, we never got lots, but there was always something – a tree and decorations and cakes and pies and a big rooster to eat. It was a time of happiness, of joy, and the festivities were pure rapture. We didn't know we weren't the richest people in the world, for all of our friends in our world had the same good times as we did and no more no less good fortune.

21

Dad made tables for dolls and sleds and wheelbarrows that could go so fast. Mom made doll beds, dresses, and blankets like no one else and hair ribbons and mittens just came automatically. Sometimes now, I'm disappointed because I feel something missing in Christmas – not that I don't receive many expensive and useful gifts from my too-generous kids. But guess it has to be I miss my childhood and the nostalgia of those long-ago Christmases.

But as all kids do, I grew up – sort of ugly and stubborn as they come, dumb also; never finished 8th grade as I quit before my 8th year was out. I learned to play the guitar (a little) when I was an early teen and when I was 16, Bill bought me a new one. Was I ever thrilled! We had lots of fun too, we'd go to other teenagers' houses and sing till late at night and then walk home for miles and miles, then get up and walk to Sunday School. We never knew when to stop.

But somehow girls aren't happy til they've broken down some guy's resistance, so in 1939, I was married to Thomas Lowry. I was 19 and he was 24. We lived on a couple of farms where we farmed on the shares, then in 1942, we moved to his grandfather's farm at Buck, where we still reside. We had four children, two boys and two girls, and raised two grandchildren. (*Editor's note: Thomas died in July 1995. Christine died in January 2021.*)

Christine and Thomas Lowry, 1975

To Tom
June 1943

He didn't fight on Corregidor,
Nor either on Bataan,
He didn't retreat in the Philippines,
Or with MacArthur stand.

He didn't fight with guns or knives,
From Berlin to Japan,
He isn't in a bomber crew.
He's just my farmer man.

He tills the soil from morn 'til night.
He works from sun to sun.
He faithfully stays with crop and herd,
'Til summer's work is done.

He may never be cited for bravery,
But he's brave and good and true.
He may wear no medals for valor,
When at last his work is through.

I pray he'll never fight in this war.
He's doing the best he can,
By doing his part in the fields all day,
And being my farmer man.

Betty

'Nuff said about me, now it's Betty's turn. She was born in 1924 in the same house where I was born at Flat Top. She was Daddy's pet when she was small, and no one dared touch her when he was around. But needless to say, he wasn't around much, so I expect she got her share of the spankings and teasing the rest of us got. I can't remember too much of her real young days as I wasn't too much older, but I remember she played by herself a lot, was very creative and still is. She was always trying new ideas, was very neat, was taller and heavier than I was when we grew up. But we courted together, which helped us to get to go more. She had a pretty alto voice and sang with Bill and I and the years rolled away as years have a way of doing and in May 1943, Betty married her only real sweetheart, Howard Fleshman. He was Tom's best friend, so that made us doubly "akin." We've had lots of fun together, cried together, raised our kids together and now our grandkids.

They moved to Washington state in 1947 and we missed them terribly, guess they missed us also, for they came home and settled in Alderson where they reside still. Howard is retired from public work, but is busy and Betty still makes pretty things and is very active in church work. She babysits the whole city of Alderson, in her "spare" time. Wish I'd got some of her talents. (*Editors note: Howard died in 2007. Betty died in 2014.*)

Front row: Bill Hodge, Bill the dog, Bill Fleshman.
Back row: Howard Fleshman, Betty Hodge, Hattie Lowry, Christine Hodge, and Thomas Lowry

Bonnie

Bonnie came along in 1929 during a big, big snow. We were living near Streeter then (still following the saw dust trail). Dad left home in the night to come to Hinton, which seemed like a long journey off, to find a doctor. The telephone lines were down and he was a long time finding one, but on the way down Beech Run Mountain, someone's cow had wandered into the road and laid down. Dad hit her with the car and killed her.

Sometime that night, he found Dr. Stokes (a new one in town). He brought him back and about daylight, we got a new sister. She was healthy, robust from the start, pretty with dark hair and brown eyes.

I was going on 9 and when school was out, she became my "project." I carried her for endless hours and saw to it that she was taken care of. She was so pretty with her dark eyes and hair and had a birthmark on the left side of her head that drew everyone's attention until her hair grew over it. She was the only one of us girls to graduate from high school, but she was and is a worker and doesn't give up and has worked in a lot of jobs. She married Edgar Lilly of Forest Hill and raised four boys. They have lived all their married life near Edgar's old homeplace and most of their family live near them. (*Editor's note: Edgar died in 1999. Bonnie died in 2021. She was the last of the Hodge siblings.*)

Melva

Melvie (Melva) was born in the Webb "holler" in 1931, a sickly baby and a sickly child. She had curly hair as a baby, which none of us had ever had, loved to sing and rock, was always pretending to be performing on the Grand Ole Opry. She was left at home with Mom and Dad after all the rest were married and stayed with them 'til in her twenties. She married Ed Meadows and moved to Wisconsin then to Michigan City, Indiana, where she still lives. She had a set of twin girls, two more boys, and two girls besides. (*Editor's note: Melva died in 2007 in Indiana.*)

Leola Bess

The youngest, Leola Bess, was born when Mom was 43 years old. A beautiful, brown-eyed, brown-haired girl. She was an angel in this life and lived three years and two months. She left us to be a real angel in Heaven. She died with spasmodic croup.

In Loving Memory of Leola Bess Hodge

3 years, 2 months, and 2 days old
Born October 3, 1933, Died December 5, 1936

An angel stepped into our home,
A short four years to stay,
She only came to win our love,
And then was called away.

Her mission here on earth was filled,
She came to show us love,
Then hurried back to Heaven,
To live with God above.

I wonder if she misses us,
Or if she is content,
To live up there instead of here,
Where a short three years were spent.

I wonder if she lifts her voice,
In that great choir to sing,
Or if she only listens,
While other voices ring.

Soon, we shall see our sister dear,
And kneel around the throne.
We'll never be homesick again,
When God calls, we'll all go home.

Date and names of this crowd of Hodges is uncertain.

L-R Christine, Bernice, Irene, and Betty

Ted

Before I go further in my story, I want to dwell awhile on my brothers. I had four that grew up along with me and no two of them were alike in much respect. Ted the oldest, five years my senior, was small and dapper like our maternal grandfather and full of Lucifer himself. He played tricks on everyone, even his elders, which was a no-no in our day. And his teachers bore the brunt of his mischief and his younger siblings were the sounding board for all his antics. He'd get us all involved and then, when we got caught, he was so innocent, and the rest of us got our hides tanned.

I guess I had a little of the devil in me also, for he and I were inseparable and I was forever in trouble. Once, when he was a world-hardened man of 14 – he dared me to take a taste of Dad's chewing tobacco. Not one to let my big brother know I wasn't game, I sneaked the plug out and put some in my mouth. Then, he took a sizable chew and said, now, if you tell on me, I'll tell on you, which was the reason I was elected in the first place, but in my innocent state, I didn't realize then.

Another time, we were older and I should have been wiser, we found a hen's nest in the weeds, with lots of eggs

– rotten of course. So, our hero climbed an old gate post and we reached the eggs up to him as he went in a mumbo jumbo of magic words as we stared up at him. He cracked the rotten eggs on the post. Needless to say, my mouth open in awe, I received a splat in the mouth and all over, to make me sicker than I remembered being up to that time.

He became a lady's man and did a lot of courting between 15 and 17, but the one and only caught him when was 18 or 19. He married Wanda Hartwell and fathered 6 children in 7 years. Times were hard then in the 1930s and he worked awful hard to provide for them but they were healthy and happy. At this writing, they moved to Virginia in the forties. He was killed in an auto accident in '85.

Bill

The next brother was Billie, though he never wanted his name other than just Bill. He was two years, two months older than I and by far, the healthiest of the brood. He bore the brunt of Ted's pranks more than any of us, because he was very cowardly of the dark when he was small, and Ted's greatest delight was to scare him out of his wits.

He was more collective than the rest of us and though times were so hard, he always managed to have some treasure the rest of us envied. He of all the boys was inclined to the culinary art and was always trying to cook something. I remember camping trips – generally an hour long – he'd build a fire and put strips of fat back on a wire and roast it in the blazes and make corn cakes to go with it. And lots of nights, I followed him through the woods and carried an oil lantern to go possum hunting – hoping to get out of drying supper dishes, which were always waiting when we got back.

I remember, once, Bill had baked cornbread, using the last of the meal, while Mom was out picking blackberries. He made an error of some sort that produced a scolding when she got in. He was very upset and cried easily. Anyway, he got out his belongings to leave home and family behind. I can see it yet, the 50 years and more have passed – he had a navy blue pullover sweater with an orange band around the neck, a pair of long johns, and a fountain pen, he traded up somewhere. He laid them out to get a box or bag to put them in and the pen leaked all over the long johns. That ended the departure. It was August anyway, and I don't think he needed the long johns.

He grew to be the Don Juan of the boys and left a trail of broken-hearted females. He spent awhile in the CCC camp then was married to Hattie Lowry on his 21st birthday. He spent some time in the navy. They had three daughters, then separated. He married Dorthy Mints and is living in Florida 25 years now. He works for Pratt Whitney Aircraft Company and is happy, healthy, and prosperous. (*Editors note: Bill died in 2012*).

Alvie

Alvie was born soon after me and we were so near the same size and age that lots of people thought we were twins. He was an awful stubborn boy and got himself into trouble with his teachers, but I'd stand behind him and try to help him out. And at home, I tried to keep him from getting whippings, which he got lots of. He was the industrious one and worked for everyone. We picked raspberries for 5 cents a gallon, for Hayden Hartwell. He hoed corn and did all kinds of tasks to keep going in those hard times.

He was drafted into the army when WWII came along and we were a broken-hearted family. He was in Italy and North Africa and a lot of dangerous places, but finally came home. When it was all over, he was married to Mabel Gautier but reenlisted and spent 20 years in the army. He went to Korea during the conflict there. He fathered three children and spent his remaining service years at Fort Meade, MD. Though ill in health and three heart attacks behind him, he works as an electrician and is still in Maryland. (*Editor's note: Alvie died in 2008.*)

Paul

The first year I started school was in 1926 and in December, I got my last baby brother, Paul, on a cold snowy night. He was delivered by a self-taught midwife – my dad being miles and miles away at a sawmill camp in Mercer County. But nevertheless, nature waits not on absent fathers or horseback doctors, snow, ice, sleet, or hail. So sometime before midnight, the angry cry of a newborn was a welcome sound to all our listening ears, and we rushed out of bed to see him get his first bath.

Dad traded our little farm at Upland for a Chevy car and we moved back to Toad Level for the ump-teenth time. Mom hadn't been to town for so long and my small brother's wardrobe lacked anything other than everyday essentials, so Mom made him a wee cap out of the top of a lady's cotton stocking adorned with blue ribbons, rosettes and ties. So began his pilgrimage by wagon to Hinton and from there by car.

We lived in a vast assortment of sawmill camps from then as the mill began to move to first one tract of timber, then another. While we lived on a farm near Streeter, Paul was two. We were playing in the barn and somehow, he ran a pitchfork into one of his eyes. He suffered terribly and lost most of the vision in that eye. He was mechanically minded and built many sawmills. (*Editors' note: Paul died in 1992.*)

The following is the exact text written on the back of this photo: First Row - Joe Pitzer - holding Tom P., Ruth Meador, Billy Hodge, Geneva Meador, Irene Hodge, Claude Meador. 2nd Row: Christine H. "Sis" Georgie Pitzer, Jewel Meador holding Martin M., Mildred Meadows (Sitting) Nellie Meadows – Bernice Hodge holding Alvie H. Back Row: Ted Hodge, Bruce Pitzer, George Pitzer holding Fred, Lettie Meador

Stories and Poetry of the Family

Christmas 1975
In loving memory of Mom and Dad

This was Mama's time of year,
The ice, the snow, the mirth.
She gave to all within her reach,
A portion of Christ's birth.

She stitched and sewed and wrapped and tied,
With loving tender care.
No needy child or lonely one
Was forgotten in her prayer.

Dad gave us all his tender care,
And saw that we were blessed.
His only wish that each of us,
Shared Christmas happiness.

Some day and soon, we'll meet again,
To share the joy and glee.
With all those gone on before
Around God's Christmas tree.

The Little Village of Buck

(Editor's note: When Christine and Thomas married, they settled in the small community of Buck, which is between Hinton and Forest Hill, WV.)

The little village of Buck on Little Wolf Creek in the 1930s was a picture of rural life at its best, calm and contented.

It boasted of two churches, a post office, a parsonage, and a two-room school. There were many farms dotting the landscape, neat and well-kept. It was overall a farming community. Everyone plowed, planted, and harvested. They had cows, horses, hogs, and some sheep, lots of chickens, and best of all, many children.

They worked long hours, and no one considered himself better than his neighbor, as each one did the same kind of work, day after day, year after year.

Everyone was his neighbor's friend, and a friend indeed, in time of trouble. If a man or one of his family were sick, the men gathered up to cut his corn, put up his hay, or cut his winter supply of wood. The ladies also cooked, cleaned, washed and ironed, and took care of the children as was necessary.

If there was a death in the community, the men left their work to dig his grave, then donned their best clothes to carry the deceased to their final resting place. The church was the hub of the community, and when six days of labor was done, everyone went to church, young and old alike. They had fellowship with their neighbors and enjoyed a day of worship.

Besides the Baptist church, there was a little Methodist church across the road. Parts of the congregation belonged to each church, that made no different to anyone. Wherever the service was, everyone worshipped together and there was no conflict. Every other year, Sunday school was held at the Baptist Church, the next year at the Methodist.

It's impossible to write about the growth of a church without mentioning the people who carried on the work of the church. There were many who worked hard to keep the churches both going during the "lean" years.

Our young people were an inspired group and many of them took on the responsibilities at an early age. They held youth meetings, and also were helpful in prayer meetings. They kept the churches clean and wood fires going in the winter months. Some of them became Sunday school teachers. During the Korean conflict as well as the World War II earlier, many of our young men were gone. The church people gathered often and prayed much for their safety.

What the church is all about is unity in heart, mind, and body. "United we stand, divided we fall" has long been a symbol or slogan. It is as true for our church, our government, or our country.

Acts, chapter 2, tells us that on the day of the Pentecost, they were all gathered in one place, of one accord. The Holy Spirit descended that day and 3000 souls were added to the church. Togetherness of one heart and one accord is what the church is all about.

One Lord God.

One faith – in Christ's finished work on Calvary.

One baptism – by the holy spirit.

Christine illustrated a story about lambs.

A Tribute to the Green Machine

(better known as the old truck) Written for Steven Lowry

Since Henry Ford first gave him birth,
He's carried many a load, twixt Heaven and Earth
Of wood, or calf or bales of hay.
He worked real hard to earn his pay.
A tank of gas, and a drink of oil
Was all he asked, for a day of toil.

When first he saw the light of day,
His paint was new, (and green they say)
But now he's rusty, and battered too;
Though his spirit's still as good as new.
Many a night when most were asleep
He pulled on home, tho the snow lay deep.
His motor worn, his lights agleam
He longed for rest, that Green Machine.

Sometimes he slipped into a ditch,
Then Steve would call him a (son-of-a-gun)
But never once was he ornery or mean
He would climb right out, that Green Machine.
He gave his best at every pull
Though loaded down with cow or bull.
He hummed right on, with a head of steam,
Never a falter, that Green Machine.

When at least his work is done,
And he's retired from his earthly run,
And settled down for his final rest,
We all can say, he did his best.
As he rolls through the Pearly Gate,
And St. Peter says, what's this? You're late?
I can hear him say with a smile and a beam.
I've never been late, I'm the Green Machine.

Stories and Poetry of Celebrations

September

September comes with book and rule,
And calls the children back to school.
Down street and lane, they hurry all,
Obedient to the school bell's call.

The shouts of playtime seems to be,
To awaken chords of memory.
I seem from some long-vanished shore,
To hear the school bells ring once more.

The school in which I am enrolled,
By which my life is now controlled,
Calls not with books, it only waits,
With labor written on its gates.

I hope to learn along the way,
Until examination day,
Great teacher keep me at thy feet,
Until my lessons are complete.

Graduation Day (Version 1)

Written for Carolyn Meadows (and later repurposed for Rhonda Kessler, Cheryl Lowry, and Candy Lilly, and probably others)

The years have swiftly passed away
We've reached the goal at last
We leave our student fellowmen
Assignments all are past.

Our Books we pass as torches
To you come behind
Hold high these swords of Knowledge
Write bold this page of time.

We march to new horizons
The drums of battle beat
We face the Call, the Challenge
We'll never sound retreat

The bells for us are silent
Our work at last is done
We leave with fond remembrance
Class Completed-eighty-one.

Graduation Day (Version 2)

O, time stand still, just for today
Let tomorrow wait – around the corner
Like a mischievous child.

O happy carefree childhood, where did you go?
On butterfly wings to some enchanted land;
To wait till I am old and live in dreams,
Will you return to warm my heart.

Will I wander again, barefoot in the dew of morning,
To the garden swing to soar far above imaginary clouds
To heights only I can scale?

Will I climb, once more the apple tree
That reaches in my childish imagination,
Far above the world below me.
Where only I can see the far horizons
And hear the challenging call of the unknown future.

O, youth with all thy dreams, the challenge,
The determination you have carried me on day by day
With the tide, til at last I am adrift.

Untitled – Unfinished "Months"

January brings the snow

The cherry hearth, the candle glow

February much the same

Sleighing parties, fireside games

In March, the wind blows, high and loud

As April pouts behind the clouds

Her showers bring the flowers gay

Their fragrance sweeten gentle May.

Cool summer nights, a sweetheart moon

Brides and roses means it's June.

Christine illustrated the poem, Come, Little Leaves by George Cooper.

What the Christmas Tree Means to Me
(a copy of this piece was also found titled The First Christmas Tree)

The Christmas tree has long been a debated subject in Christian homes all over America, as some would suggest it to be an object of idolatry. After pondering over the possibility or impossibility of that idea, a story came to me; it is only a figment of my imagineation and certainly would bear record. But let me tell of a story that come to me from an old, old, man many years ago:

It seems that because of his Christian beliefs, he was forced to leave his home one cold wintry Christmas Eve and in searching for a shelter out of a raging snow storm, he crawled underneath the weighted branches of a snow-laden fir tree. The thick branches were laden with snow and drooped almost to the ground. Soon he discovered, he was not alone for the limbs of the tree were full of feathered and furred creatures also seeking refuge from the storm and in its shelter they were safe. Soon all were asleep while outside the storm raged on, but in the night the ceased, the moon and stars broke through the clouds and awakened the old man. Looking up through the branches, it seemed that a giant star rested atop the tree and glittering moonlight made the tree aglow as tho it were covered in beautiful lights and underneath the quietest and peaceful solitude of warmth and shelter.

The old man gazed at the beauty of that early Christmas morning, feeling refreshed and happy to have see and been a part of that first Christmas tree.

For as he told his story many times he said: The lowering branches reminded me of my Savior's arms, shielding me from all harm, as the storms of life raged on. The star atop the tree reminded me of the star that led the shepherds and the wise men, when they came in search of the Christ child. The starlight glittering on the branches reminds me of the colors of all the jewels I shall see when I reach heaven and last of all the evergreen of the tree reminds of me of that eternal city where I shall live and never die. The creatures that shared the shelter of the tree with me, remind me of all those friends and loved ones I shall see at last. The evergreen tree itself reminds me of that eternal city, where I shall live and never die.

So when you gather with your loved ones around your Christmas tree, remember the old man's story and how we came to have the decorated tree at Christmas to commemorate the birth of him who came that we might have life eternal.

Stories and Poetry of Patriotism

Happy Birthday, West Virginia, June 20, 1976

I am West Virginia and today is my birthday. I am 113 years old.

My mother country gave me birth, while she suffered the pangs of a great civil war. I was very small, but I have become very strong. Through my veins run rich seams of coal, natural gas, oil, and the clear sparkling rivers and streams. On my face are large dairy farms, apple orchards, wheat, corn, and hay fields. My forests are filled with virgin timbers. My cities and towns are alive with factories and mills. My parks and playgrounds, lakes, and mountain peaks afford pleasure to sports men from all over the world.

My people are the greatest people on earth, proud because they have so much, yet humbly thankful because they have so much to share with those who have not. Many thousand of my young people have answered the call to arms, when danger threatened my mother country. Many of them never came back, yet freely gave their life blood, that we might remain free.

My children are scattered to the four corners of the earth, yet they always find their way home; for here, on my hills are their roots, here where man can walk hand in hand with God and nature.

I snuggle contentedly between my sister states, and say to myself, Happy Birthday old girl, you've come a long way.

Our Heritage
June 1981

Two hundred years and more have passed
Since men this nation sought.
To gain the freedom that they lacked
With blood, this nation bought.

Undaunted courage, strength of steel
They built this nation strong.
Nor faltered when the day grew dark
But sang the Victor's song.

Again, we need such men as they
To lead this nation through.
We can't fall back, we must go forth
We'll prove God's word is true.

We'll let our cry forever be
"In God we Trust," and then,
The praise and honour all be his
And not to mortal man.

While men and nations strive for naught,
Lord, let our faith be strong
When earthly riches all are past
And all their strength is gone.

If we join hands and kneel in prayer,
And ask his will be done
In hearts and lives around the world
The victory shall be won.

Carter's Peanut Patch

When I was young and in my prime
And the election rolled around,
I searched for a likely Candidate
And a strange one I found;
He was big and tall, had a southern drawl
And never wore a hat.
He said, vote for me and I'll take you free
To my Georgia Peanut Patch

Well, he got in the boat, and I cast my boat
The very first thing you know,
That peanut picker was in Washington
Doing a brand-new show
He said, I'll raise your wage, I'll cut your tax
I'll take you where it's at, you voted for me,
Now it's plain to see you're an heir
To a Peanut Patch

Well, some people go to the old folk's home
Or the poor house on the hill
Some people take their pensions, in hundred-dollar bills.
It's not for me, as you can see, I'm going where it's at
Gonna live in peace, gonna take my ease
In my Georgia Peanut Patch

You've heard of Carters underwear and Carter's liver pills
You've heard of Carters oats I know and now it's Carters
bills
He wants legal Marijuana and bills for this and that
But the only thing that interests me,
Is Carters Peanut Patch

He said, we need no tanks or guns, we need no B-1 plane
We'll live in peace with our enemies
And we'll take all the blame.
When our work is done, we'll go down south
And live just where it's at
When the Russians land, we'll take 'em by the hand
And lead to our Peanut Patch

Chorus:
Oh, a peanut patch in Georgia, that's where I'm gonna be
When my work is done and my race is won,
I'm going there you see
When I've done my time, down here on earth,
I'm going where it's at
Gonna live in peace, gonna take my ease,
In a Georgia Peanut Patch

Psalm of the Hills

God surely must have smiled
When he made the West Virginia hills!
As he molded out the valleys, the rivers and the dells,
He took His mighty paintbrush and splashed an autumn hue.
Then gilded it with sunshine and sweetened it with dew.

He filled a thousand mountain streams with perch, trout, and
bass,
And made a shady nook for me with elm and sassafras.
He sprinkled diamond dust in the heavens up above,
And in each twinkling light, sends a messages, God is Love!

He spreads an ermine carpet when winter's ground is bare.
And in the spring, each tree will wear a robin in her hair.
A softly sighing night wind lulls your soul to rest
And to see a mountain sunrise is to know that you are blessed.

Roam the U.S.A all the way to the golden gate,
Hill country memories will bring you home to our state.
You've heard the angels sing once you hear the whippoorwill,
Cause God puts a little heaven in every West Virginia hill.

Thank God for America 1976

This piece was written in 1976, but Christine then later submitted a slightly revised version to the Hinton News as a letter to the editor on December 26, 2001 with the following note:

Dear Editor, I wrote the enclosed "Thought for today," and thought it might be a good note for all the troubles and worries of today – to set aside a few moments – and give thought to how thankful we should be. Hope you can find a corner somewhere in the paper next week.

How thankful we should be this bicentennial year, not just on Thanksgiving day, but every day of the year, for the freedom we share as a nation.

This nation was founded by those to whom freedom meant more than life, they were willing to give their lives that their children and generations to come could know freedom, and because of their determination, their faithfulness and complete trust in God, God blessed this nation and set it free.

This nation of ours nestled between two mighty oceans, is the greatest nation on earth, we have freedom from want, from fear or bondage.

Our children are happy and carefree. They've never heard the roar of war planes in the night, the screaming missiles and exploding bombs. They've never known the terror of enemy tanks in the street, of marching soldiers with bayonets ready. They've never known fear of the guillotine or concentration camps or breadlines or empty stomachs. They've never known hunger or disease without medicine.

How humble our prayers should be this Thanksgiving day 1976, that a few people more than two hundred years ago were willing to step out, to stand up and fight for the freedom this country enjoys.

The freedom to speak out for what we believe in, the freedom to worship the true God of Glory, wherever and whenever we choose.

The freedom and the blessing to lay down to rest at the close of day and say, "Thank you, God for this nation and the privilege to be an American."

The Best Thing About WV is:

First, the best thing about WV is it is Home—It is home to me and my family, our relatives and friends. It is home to many hardworking, honest, kind, gentle people who have made WV what it is. A state to be proud of, A state that is rich in history in resources and legends.

It is home to thousands of wildlife species, sheltered by the cool leafy forests, by the fields and watered by the clear sparkling water of rivers and streams. It is home to; hundreds of birds who also nest and feed in the trees and fields.

The next best thing about WV is the freedom we feel, the security and the peace, that lets us lie down at night with no threat of terrorism, no riots in the streets no uprisings that brings fear to hearts, no fear of gang wars or bombings.

The freedom of speech, the freedom we have to have a voice in our government and in our schools and work places. The freedom to choose our place to work and play, our place of worship and the freedom to choose our politics or religion. The freedom from want, the right to work as we choose to fill our needs, the right to till the soil, to plant and harvest. The right to seek the knowledge of our capacity to further our education if we so desire and are willing to work for our goals.

Yes, WV has been home to a lot of people, many left behind a legend of heroic deeds and the heritage they left for us is a challenge to hold high the torch, to carry proudly the banner to sing the victor's song and be proud to be West Virginians for the best thing about WV is: It is HOME.

A sketch of the WV Seal that Christine used for a pattern for a WV history quilt.

Stories and Poetry of Faith

The Miracle Man
February 1973

Jesus Christ was a man of miracles. He came into the world as a miracle; his birth was a miracle birth, insomuch that he was born of a virgin and was the only begotten son of God.

He also went out of this world as a miracle. His life was one continuous miracle. He healed the blind eyes, the deaf ears, and restored life to the dead. His miracles still exist today, when men will believe that he is.

The shackles of sin will fall, the sinful habit of a lifetime will vanish, and eyes blinded to the things of God will be opened to new light and new understanding, Ears that have been deaf to the good news of the gospel will hear anew the old, old story of this miracle man.

Jesus Christ; He was a living miracle because he lived a miracle life, disappearing many times when men sought to take his life. He was a miracle man because the cross could not obliterate him, the grave could not hold him, and the miracle of it all is, He lived.

The cross for him was just a stepping stone between Earth and heaven, for us who will believe in this man of miracles, Jesus Christ.

Outside Looking In

(A song inspired by a sermon delivered by Pastor Don Hannah at the Little Wolf Creek Baptist Church)

Would you like to be standing where you could look inside,
Heaven's portals when the stars come out tonight?
Would you like to see Jesus who gave his life for you?
See the saints all in their glory shining bright?

Would you like to see St. Matthew, Mark, and Luke and John?
Would you like to see the golden streets that they new walk upon?
Would you like to stroll with them along the avenue?
If you waste your life in sinful things, you'll never make it through.

Chorus:
Will you be on the inside looking out, or be on the outside looking in?
If you waste your life in pleasure and cling to things of sin,
You'll be standing on the outside, looking in.

When God told old Noah to go and build the ark
He told him he would shut the saved ones in
But those who wouldn't listen, and mocked this man of God,
Would be standing on the outside looking in.

When the rain came pouring down and mighty was the wind,
The people cried in anguish, Old Noah let us in.
But just as God had promised, the door was closed within
And those who wouldn't listen, were outside looking in.

When Jesus died on Calvary, he opened up the road
That we could walk inside the blessed way.
But to those who will not listen and waste their life in sin
Will be standing on the outside when the door is closed again.

He is not here: But is Risen!
Easter Program 1994

It is Easter time again, a time when earth is renewing itself, with the green of spring time.
When the singing of birds and bright flowers blooming tell us it is a time of new beginnings.

A time when we pause to meditate and go back through the pages of history to retrace the footsteps of our Lord as he walked the lonely road to Calvary.

He who could have called 10,000 angels to carry him away, yet he chose to go alone, obediently to the cross that God's purpose for the salvation of mankind might be fulfilled.

He died alone forsaken by friends and in his dying hour his Father turned his face from him because of the sing he bore on the cross for us.

In the darkest hour ever recorded on the pages of time, when in agony of body and soul, he cried out, "It is finished", The work he came to earth to do was done, forever settled.

Those who would like to forever obliterate him still cry, "Away with him!" Wipe his name from the written page! Take his teachings out of the class room. His influence out of the churches, out of the home forever, blot out this name of all names!

This Easter let each of us have a new beginning, Let us be willing to love hime, to serve him, to witness every day for him, The message of the angels on that first Easter morn. "The Lord is risen indeed! And is alive forever more."

I was the One

'Way out on a hill, to a place called Mt. Calvary.
Jesus was led to die on a cross
Wounded and weary, despised and rejected.
He took the place of a world that was lost.

The crowds gathered 'round him, with loud accusations.
There was no one to aid him, his friends had all gone.
The multitude cried out, let's crucify Jesus.
Ready and willing, I was the one.

(Chorus)
Yes, I was the one, who crucified Jesus.
I drove the nails through his feet and his hands.
I drew the sword that spilled out his life blood.
Oh, Lord, please forgive me, for I was the one.

Dying alone, by friends all forsaken.
There was no one to ease the pain that he bore.
I saw the blood drops grow red on his forehead.
Caused by the thorns in the crown that he wore.

I tossed the dice that parted his garments.
All that he owned for this world to see.
At the foot of the cross, I reach for my portion,
But a drop of his blood spilled down upon me.

Down on my knees, I looked up at Jesus.
His eyes were wide open, yet his life had all gone.
I saw the love and gentle compassion.
I saw forgiveness for the deeds I had done.

The Ox Yoke
1973

The path through the forest was uneven and rocky. The trees, such as they were, were gnarled and crooked, as if the soil on which they had their beginnings were starved for lack of nutrition. But day after day the barefoot boy came along the forest path searching for just the right timber to be used for the task at hand in the humble carpenter shop.

He was sturdy, yet gentle and his voice was smooth and tender. He always seemed busy and excited, yet never seemed tired as he searched through the trees. A crooked, bent little tree grew just away from the path through the forest and try as he might to grow upright, he remained gnarled and twisted and never seemed to be quite tall enough to see the owner of the tender-voiced man child. He wished with all his crooked little heart that just once he could grow tall enough to see him.

Every day as the sun kissed the hillsides good morning, he would stretch and bend this way and that to catch the warmth of the morning sun, hoping it would make him grow above the rugged growth that surrounded him. And when night came down on the Palestinian countryside, he would not to the first little stars and try as hard as he could to reach up and out. Maybe tomorrow would be the day he would be just tall enough to see the owner of the voice that came to the forest.

But when another day would come, he was just as bent and twisted as before. Then one day the voice came closer and closer, and suddenly the little tree was trembling as though a sudden breeze had come up from Galilee, for the owner of the voice was looking on him with the kindest eyes he'd ever imagined and the gentle hands

68

were lifting him as thought he'd been a newborn lamb and carried him out of the forest where he'd spent his entire life. But the little tree quivered happily to be going with the boy, who was so strong and yet so gentle.

He was set down at last at the door to a carpenter shop and the voice of the boy was excited as he described the shape of the twisted little tree to the bearded man inside. The days passed and gentle hands rubbed and polished the crooked little tree till he felt very special, though he wasn't sure why but somehow, he knew he was meant for a special mission.

One day he felt he was ready for whatever he was intended for. Tender hands carried him outside to where cattle waited and he was lifted carefully to the shoulders of two young oxen. The twisted limbs of the little tree had been bent at just the right angle to make a yoke for the young oxen. Whatever magic the yoke possessed, he felt must have come the gentle hands that had reshaped his life, for when the stubborn little oxen wore the yoke, they always walked where they were supposed to walk and did their work well.

No matter how twisted and bent our bodies or our lives have grown, the gentle hands of the man from Galilee can reshape and remold us to be useful vessels for whatever work he wants us to do.

Three Crosses
1997

Upon a rugged windswept hill
Three crosses bleak and bare
And down below the angry cries
Of hatred fill the air

Away with him, let's crucify
The crowd in anger cry
He says he is the Son of God
Blasphemers have to die.

Then Jesus Christ, the Lamb of God
Was led to Pilate's hall
Abused and beaten, spit upon
And scourged before them all.

But still he answered not a word
When asked if he had said
That he was Christ, the Son of God,
The Life, the living bread.

I find no fault, then Pilate said,
Chastise and set him free
But still, the angry mob cried out
Let's nail him to a tree.

He could have called to Heaven's throne
And asked they all to be gone
But still obedient unto death
He said, "Thy will be done."

Then on his head, they placed a crown
Of cruel and piercing thorns
And on his back, a purple robe
To mock him and to scorn.

He took the cross, that bore our sins
And climbed old Calvary's hill
And there between two dying thieves
He did his Father's will.

My work is finished now he said
That all men might be free
He bore it all that we might live
With him, eternally.

Why a Manger Instead of a Mansion

Why did the baby Jesus come,
To a manger for his bed
No room in the inn, they were told,
Just a lowly cattle shed.

Why did the angels come that night,
To the humblest of men,
To announce the birth of a newborn king
Who would save the world from sin.

Why wasn't a room prepared for him,
In the palace of the king
With softest pillows, velvet spread.
While Heaven's angels sang.

The prophets had told the story,
Of the place of Jesus' birth
And how he would come as a servant
To teach the men on Earth.

God knew King Herod was wicked,
His heart as hard as stone
No room in his palace for a little babe
Who would someday inherit a throne.

So Christ still comes to sinful men
He cares for everyone
He has a mansion waiting,
When life on Earth is done.

Jesus was Walking with Me (2012)

I was walking alone in the night.
I looked all around me, but I saw no light.
I felt a presence but none could I see.
Jesus was walking with me.

He stepped up beside me,
And reached for my hand,
He said, let me lead you
Through life's sinking sand.
I saw the nail prints,
He had suffered for me,
Jesus was walking with me.

He still walks beside me,
Through the long years
His presence still leads me
Through heartache and tears.
When the beauty of heaven
At last, I shall see.
He will be waiting for me.

Standing at the Crossroad
October 1975

Many long years, I wandered in sin,
Never inviting the dear Savior in,
Ruining my future, wasting my life,
That's how I came to the crossroad one night.

Standing at the crossroads, the broad road I see,
Bright lights and music beckoning to me,
But down on my knees, I feel by the way,
That night at the crossroad, I learned how to pray.

A nail scarred hand that night I could see,
Reaching in mercy and pardon for me.
That's when I traded the wrong for the right,
When I met Jesus at the crossroad that night.

He showed me his side that was wounded for me,
Showed me the scars in hands and his feet.
I saw the blood from the thorns shed for me,
There at the crossroad, I saw Calvary.

If you are wasting the best of your life,
If you are walking in sin and in strife,
Look all around you and come to the light.
Christ at the crossroads is waiting tonight.

Untitled
2008

Lord, when you walked upon the earth,
A friend to all you met,
Please, teach me how to do the same,
That I shall not forget.

My neighbor is my brother,
Perhaps a soul in need,
Could use my help and comfort,
And be a friend indeed.

That I might share a bit of bread,
To those who may have none,
And tell them of a loving God,
And of his precious son.

Who came to earth, one starry night,
Born in a cattle stall,
And died upon a rugged cross,
To save us one and all.

Untitled

God called our loved one home to rest
Where pain will be no more
Where night nor storm can never come
Beyond the sunset shore.

He knows what's best, though we are prone
To question his great will
Remember how in waves tossed high,
He whispered, "Peace be still."

He knew that pain was hard to bear
He knew the night was long
But wasn't ready yet to call
Our precious loved one home.

But when her mission here was filled
He whispered come on home
Your place is ready here with me
Around the great white throne.

We cannot see beyond the stars
To where our loved ones wait
With outstretched hands to greet us there
Beside a golden gate.

Poetry of the Mountains

Snowflake
(February 10, 2011)

God patterned every snowflake
And even so the stars
Just as he patterned you and me
No matter who we are.

He evened out the sunbeams
That each would have a place
So every little forever plant
Would have a smiling face.

He made each of us different
And yet we are the same
He placed us here to learn of him
And praise his holy name.

Call of the Whip-poor-will

It was just an old house, sitting up on a hill
Serenaded at night, by a whip-poor-will
His plaintive call was one of love
As he called to his mate, somewhere above.

When from a far-off distant hill
She would answer the call of the whip-poor-will
With one last note, he would fly away
To be heard no more, 'til another day.

Now I sit alone in the house on the hill
I hear no voice, the house is still
The little ones in noisy play
Like the whip-poor-will have flown away.

Sometimes at night, when all is still
It seems I can hear the call of the whip-poor-will
But, then I know it is only me
Wishing for things that cannot be.

Oft in memory, I can hear all the sounds of other years
A husband home from work all day,
Children laughing at their play
But all have gone, from the house on the hill
Just like the call of the whip-poor-will.

70696009R00046